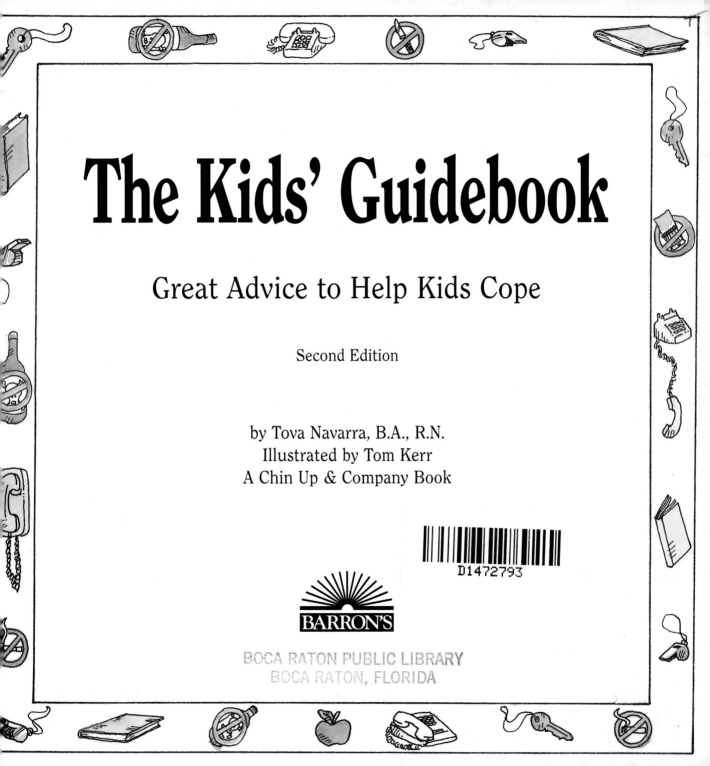

The Kids' Guidebook

Great Advice to Help Kids Cope

Second Edition

by Tova Navarra, B.A., R.N.
Illustrated by Tom Kerr
A Chin Up & Company Book

BARRON'S

Published 2002 by Barron's Educational Series, Inc.

All inquiries should be addressed to:
Barron's Educational Series, Inc.
250 Wireless Boulevard
Hauppauge, New York 11788
http://www.barronseduc.com

Library of Congress Catalog Card No.: 2002018585
International Standard Book No.: 0-7641-2066-2

Library of Congress Cataloging-in-Publication Data

Navarra, Tova.
    The kids' guidebook : great advice to help kids cope // by Tova Navarra ;
illustrated by Tom Kerr.—2nd ed.
        p.   cm.
    Rev. ed. of: On my own (1993) which was originally published as: Playing it
smart (c1989). "A Chin Up & Company book."
    Includes index.
    Summary: Offers advice for young people on how to handle a variety of situations
when an adult might not be around to help.
    ISBN 0-7641-2066-2
    1. Children—Life skills guides—Juvenile literature.   2. Self-reliance in children—
Juvenile literature.   [1. Self-reliance. 2. Safety. 3. Conduct of life.]   I. Kerr, Tom, ill.
II. Navarra, Tova. Playing it smart.   III. Title.

HQ781.N28   2002
305.23—dc21   2002018585

Printed in Hong Kong
9 8 7 6 5 4 3 2 1

TABLE OF CONTENTS

AUTHOR'S NOTE TO PARENTS

Oh, to be a child again! But children's issues today—peer pressure, broken homes, early sexual activity, molestation, and substance abuse among them—are not the same as they were even a generation ago.

I'd like to help the younger generation figure things out without the agony of trial and error. My challenge, as I saw it, was to create an opportunity for kids to focus on and set in motion their natural intelligence.

No one has all the answers. But the reality is that children do worry about things. While one of my goals was to help parents and caregivers explain touchy topics, another was to offer straightforward advice that kids can read by themselves if they're too shy, as kids often are, to ask questions.

If you read this book with your child, it provides a springboard for communication. As you become more sensitive to what bothers many children, you can discuss situations and give realistic advice *before* there's a problem. Prevention is paramount: Children who know some first-aid measures in advance can deal better with a physical crisis; children who understand why people behave certain ways and who have a few stock responses can ward off painful feelings.

You can't be there every moment for your children, but children can open this book anytime for some down-to-earth, friendly information. I hope it gives parents a much-deserved break and steers kids toward a safer and happier childhood.

IF YOU'RE HOME ALONE AND HEAR SCARY NOISES, try to figure out what they could be. There are strange sounds in every house or apartment, and most of the time they come from the refrigerator turning on and off, the furnace humming, a loose windowpane rattling, or another common source. When you are alone, you may hear sounds you don't normally notice when others are around. Do the stairs squeak? Could a tree branch be tapping against the window? Do you know what a dripping faucet sounds like?

It's easy to let your imagination get the better of you. If the normal noises still bother you, try turning on the TV, radio, or stereo. That can make you feel less nervous and drown out the other noises.

If you are sure the other noises aren't normal and could mean danger, call a neighbor, friend, or relative. Call the police first if you think someone is trying to break in. Tell the police your name and address so they can find you. They'll probably want you to stay on the phone with them, stay calm, and hide until they get there. Knowing what to do ahead of time helps you feel in control. Remember that most people who break into houses want to steal things without anyone seeing them. They usually don't plan on hurting anybody.

IF YOU GET A CUT OR SCRAPE, the first thing to do is stop the bleeding. Press firmly on the cut with a clean handkerchief or any clean cloth. That should slow the bleeding. If you don't have any cloth, you can use a paper towel or tissues. The important thing is to keep pressing until the bleeding stops. If the cut is still bleeding, cover it and press it again or wrap it firmly in cloth and call someone for help.

If the cut is not too bad and the bleeding has stopped, wash the area very gently with soap and water. Ask Mom or Dad to show you how to use a first-aid cream or spray that will kill the germs. It may sting a little, but that means it is cleaning the cut and will make sure it doesn't get infected. If you have the kind of cut that looks open, cover it with a Band-Aid. Tell Mom or Dad what happened when they get home.

If you learn what to do before you get hurt, it won't seem so bad.

IF YOU GET SOMETHING IN YOUR EYE, go to a sink and turn on the cool water. Splash cool water in your open eye many times. Whatever got in your eye may wash away.

If that doesn't work, stay calm. Don't rub your eye. That could hurt it. Walk slowly to an adult for help.

If there isn't an adult nearby and you think there may be something more serious than a speck of dirt or an eyelash, call 911 for an emergency, or 0 for Operator or the first-aid department in your area. Let Mom or Dad know what happened.

IF YOU SWALLOW SOMETHING BY ACCIDENT THAT ISN'T FOOD, call Mom, Dad, or another adult immediately. An adult can decide what kind of help you may need.

If you've swallowed something small like a penny (and you are NOT choking or feeling pain in your throat), stay calm. Dad or Mom will probably call your doctor to find out what to do. Sometimes the doctor will tell you to wait until the object passes out of your body when you go to the bathroom. Or the doctor may want you to go to the hospital for X rays. X rays are special pictures that let the doctor see what's inside of you.

If you swallow medicine, pills, soap, or anything that could be poison or could injure your throat or stomach, call the police or the poison-control number immediately. Then call Mom or Dad and let them know what happened. Lots of things around the house may be poisonous if you eat or drink them— even dishwashing detergent, hand lotion, or shampoo. Hold on to the container of anything you may have swallowed, because the doctor will want to know what it was in order to help you get better. When you are waiting for help, be still. Jumping around may make things worse. If another child has swallowed something that may be harmful, call for help, and then keep him or her quiet.

Did you ever feel little shocks of static electricity when you walk in your socks on a carpet or touch an electrical appliance a certain way? Static electricity can even make a tiny buzzing noise. This is different from the kind of shock you can get from touching an exposed electrical wire or putting a metal object like a fork or knife into a toaster or other appliance.

IF YOU GET AN ELECTRIC SHOCK FROM AN APPLIANCE, unplug the cord if you can. Don't touch the plug if wires are sticking out or you can see that the covering of the wire is open or broken. Get away from any appliance or electrical outlet or plug that begins to spark or smoke, and call the fire department immediately. Never take a foolish chance that you can deal with the situation by yourself.

Electricity can be very dangerous. It's often best to ask Mom, Dad, or another adult to help you when you want to use the toaster or plug in any appliance. Girls should be extra careful with curling irons or hair dryers. Be sure the appliance is not near water, because water allows electricity to flow through it and you could get shocked.

NEVER USE ANYTHING ELECTRICAL WHEN YOUR HANDS ARE WET OR YOU ARE NEAR WATER. Do not use an electric radio or other appliance when you are in the bathtub or shower or filling the sink with water. If a lightning storm begins when you're in a swimming pool or the tub, get out fast and dry off quickly.

If someone else is touching a wire and getting a bad shock, don't touch him or her, because you might get shocked, too. You may not hear any yelling or see any sign of trouble, but that doesn't always mean everything is fine. If a wire or appliance is causing a shock, the person may not be able to let go of it. Use a stick of wood or a wooden broom handle to help push the person away from the source of the shock. Electricity does not go through wood. Make sure there isn't any metal on the wooden pole, because electricity travels through metal very quickly. Be sure to call for help or see that anyone who receives an electric shock is taken to a doctor.

IF SOMEONE SEEMS TO BE DROWNING, yell and run for help. Don't waste a second. You might be able to get help very quickly.

It is usually not a good idea to jump into the water to try to save someone. When someone is in trouble, he is desperate. He may not be thinking clearly. He could hurt you without even realizing it. Then both of you could be in danger of drowning.

If you think you are strong enough and long tree branches or logs are near, you can move them into the water. The drowning person might be able to grab onto them and pull himself out. Or look for something that will float to throw to him. It could be a tire, a large wooden object, life jacket, chair cushion, beach ball, or even a raft.

It's very important to swim with other people. That way, someone can go for help if there is any trouble. Always swim in areas protected by lifeguards.

Never think you can play or skate on a pond, lake, or any body of water that seems to be frozen unless you see posted safety signs. And have an adult with you. You don't ever really

know where the ice may be too thin to hold you up. Stay in areas that are in clear view of other people and where others are skating. Always use the buddy system, which means skating with another person or in a group. But **IF SOMEONE HAS FALLEN THROUGH THE ICE**, stay away from the hole, even if you think you could grab onto the person and help him or her climb out. The ice around the hole may be very weak and both of you could fall through. The best thing to do is yell and run for help. After you've done that, follow the advice in the section on drowning.

Sometimes a kid thinks it's fun to do something dangerous. Don't let anyone tell you a place or activity is safe if you know it may not be. There are plenty of fun things to do without putting yourself at risk.

IF YOU TOUCH SOMETHING HOT AND GET BURNED, put the burned part under very cold water, in ice water, or, as a last resort, on something frozen right away. Putting your finger in ice water is the best first-aid measure, but anything cold will help relieve the burn. Cold helps your burn heal faster and takes away some of the stinging. Cold can also prevent a blister from forming.

If you can't make ice water, wrap a piece of ice or something frozen in a towel or piece of cloth (even a T-shirt will do) and gently dab the burn. Don't press ice against the burn for longer than a few seconds on and off. If you keep ice on it too long, the healthy skin around the burn may become injured. For a burn that's small and seems to be relieved by ice water, you can apply some aloe lotion or a sunburn spray or ointment to help the skin heal. Show the burn to an adult as soon as possible. Ask your family what first-aid treatment they keep in the house in case of a burn. If the burn is bad or large, call an adult or the emergency number for help.

Always eat at a reasonable pace and take small bites. This prevents choking on something. If you gobble up your food too fast, put too much in your mouth at once, or start to laugh or horse around while you are eating, you may be in danger of getting something stuck in your windpipe. Use your better judgment: Chew your food thoroughly before you swallow, and eat calmly. But IF YOU ARE ALONE AND START TO CHOKE on a piece of food or an object, go to an adult immediately for help. If no one is around and you are having trouble breathing, run *very hard* into something about as high or a little higher than your waist, like a table, chair, or other piece of furniture. It may hurt your chest and stomach for a while, but this action will push against your stomach and chest, force your breath out hard, and help force the food out of your windpipe or throat. This is called the Heimlich maneuver.

After you do this, call 911 or the police to make sure you will be all right. Choking can make you feel weak or faint.

Ask your parents to contact the local first-aid squad about taking a Heimlich maneuver course. You may have heard about a boy who saved a little girl's life. He knew how to do the Heimlich maneuver from watching TV and he used it to stop the girl from choking to death. Can you imagine how happy he must have felt? You may help save someone's life if you know what to do ahead of time.

Never practice the Heimlich maneuver the way you would actually do it if someone were choking. Using that much force could injure another person. Use force only in case of emergency. Remember, the Heimlich maneuver is not a game; it's a way to save a person's life.

IF YOU ARE HOME ALONE AND A FIRE STARTS, try to be calm and think quickly about what you should do. If flames or smoke are coming from the toaster, TV or other appliances, pull out the plug, but only if you can do it very fast and without getting hurt. Never put water on an electrical fire. Call the fire department. If you don't have the fire department's number handy, call 0 for Operator. Tell the operator there's a fire at your house and make sure you give your address so the firemen can find you. If you have time, close the door where the fire is so the fire doesn't spread so fast.

If a very small fire starts in the frying pan or pot on the stove, turn off the stove. Get a pot lid big enough to cover the pot or pan and put it down over the fire. Stopping air from getting to a fire puts out the flame. Water can put out most fires, but don't throw water on a stove fire. If you don't have a lid, dump a lot of salt or baking soda straight from the carton on the fire. Don't try to fight a fire that's too big to handle. Talk to Mom and Dad about how to decide if a fire is a big or a little one.

If you're in the house and a large fire starts, walk, don't run, out of the house. If smoke starts to fill the room, crawl out of the room quickly. Smoke rises, so you can probably breathe more easily on the floor. If your clothes catch on fire, lie down on the floor and roll back and forth to put out the flames. When you get outside, go to a neighbor's house right away and call the fire department. Don't stop on your way to take anything with you. Don't stop to try to rescue any pets. Just get out of the house as fast as you can. Being safe is the most important thing.

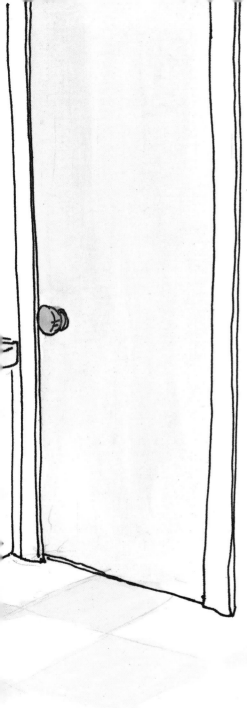

IF YOU ARE ALONE AND HAVE DIARRHEA, A STOMACHACHE, A BAD HEADACHE, OR OTHER SICK FEELING, call your parents or another adult you know and ask what you should do. Don't take any medicine that's in the house. You might take something that will make you feel worse. If you can't reach your parents or another adult you know who could help you, call 911 or your family doctor. Keep the doctor's number near the phone in case of emergency. Ask Mom or Dad what to do ahead of time in case of sickness. If you have asthma, for example, be sure to use your inhaler or take your medication the way your doctor taught you to. If you are having severe pain, difficulty breathing, or an asthma attack you think is worse than usual, call for help immediately. Knowing what to do ahead of time is best, because it will help you stay calm and think straight when you really need to.

Sometimes you can't help falling down or hitting your head on something. It happens to everyone now and then. IF YOU HIT YOUR HEAD AND FEEL A BUMP, put two ice cubes in a plastic bag and hold it on the bump for a little while, or until you feel better. If you don't have ice, take something small out of the freezer and put it on the bump or wherever it hurts. If you are outdoors, go home, to the nearest adult you know, or to a place where you can get help.

If you feel dizzy, have blurry vision, ringing in your ears, a bad headache, or you throw up after you've hit your head, call 911 immediately.

IF A TOOTH FALLS OUT, rinse your mouth out with cold water. You may bleed a little, but it will stop in just a few minutes. Show the tooth to a grown-up.
And smile! Your baby teeth are making way for your adult teeth.

IF YOU GET TO YOUR HOUSE AND FIND A DOOR OR WINDOW OPEN, don't go inside. Go immediately to a friend or relative's house. Or go back to the school if it's nearby and there are crossing guards. Ask the adult to call the police. They will come and check your house to make sure a stranger isn't inside and everything is all right.

You can call your mom or dad or the adult you're supposed to call in case of an emergency. Carry Mom's and Dad's phone numbers in your pocket or in a safe place.

IF YOUR NOSE STARTS TO BLEED, sit down and lean forward a little. Don't tilt your head back. Pinch your nostrils closed for a few minutes and breathe through your mouth. That should stop the bleeding. If the bleeding hasn't stopped, do this again for a little longer time. If the bleeding gets worse, call 911. Once the nosebleed is over, try not to blow your nose for a while. If the bleeding won't stop, call or go to an adult for help.

Don't pick at your nose. You might start the bleeding all over again.

IF YOU GET A SPLINTER, see if a piece of the splinter is sticking out. If it is, pull it straight out. Clean the spot where the splinter was with soap and water.

If the splinter is not sticking out, leave it alone until you can show it to an adult. If the splinter is very big or a piece of glass, leave it alone and go to an adult for help right away.

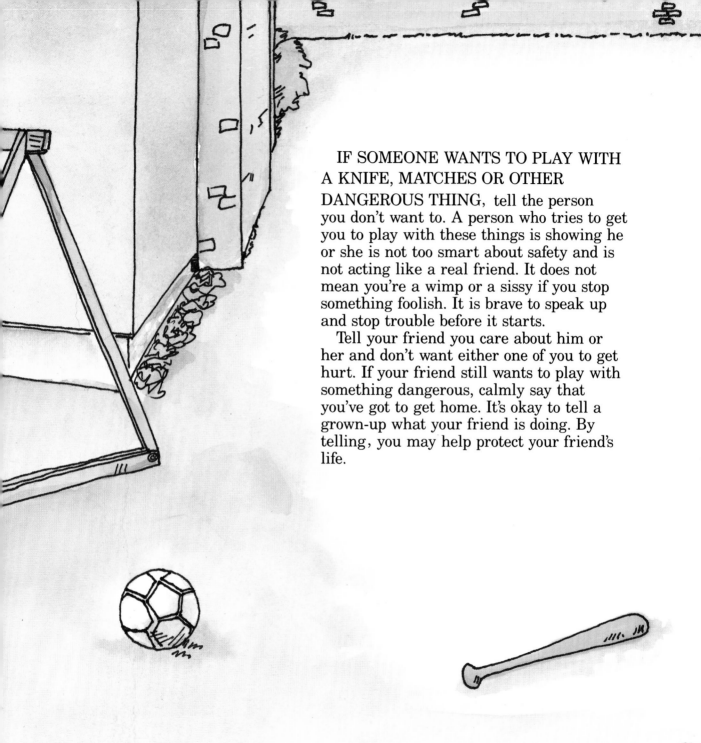

IF SOMEONE WANTS TO PLAY WITH A KNIFE, MATCHES OR OTHER DANGEROUS THING, tell the person you don't want to. A person who tries to get you to play with these things is showing he or she is not too smart about safety and is not acting like a real friend. It does not mean you're a wimp or a sissy if you stop something foolish. It is brave to speak up and stop trouble before it starts.

Tell your friend you care about him or her and don't want either one of you to get hurt. If your friend still wants to play with something dangerous, calmly say that you've got to get home. It's okay to tell a grown-up what your friend is doing. By telling, you may help protect your friend's life.

IF YOU ARE HOME ALONE AT NIGHT AND THE ELECTRICITY GOES OUT, stay where you are if you are comfortable. You may bump into things and hurt yourself if you start moving around in the dark. A blackout usually lasts only a little while, so be patient.

If you have a flashlight, call your parents on the phone or call the person they expect you to call in an emergency. Don't light matches or candles. If you can get to your room easily, get in bed and relax until the lights come back on. You can listen to the radio if it works on batteries.

Keep a flashlight with fresh batteries where you can get to it in the dark. The entire family should know where the flashlight is kept.

If you think the lights went out because of a problem in the house, call the police. Maybe you saw sparks fly, heard a strange noise, or smelled something burning. Don't use electrical appliances or anything with a plug.

Before a blackout happens, talk to your parents about what you should do.

IF A STRANGE DOG COMES NEAR YOU, keep very calm. The dog is probably just curious and wants to sniff you. That's how a dog gets to know people. If the dog thinks you're not afraid, he'll probably just sniff at you and then go away. Don't shake your hands or make sudden moves. He may look friendly, but you shouldn't try to pet him. Let the dog walk away from you. Then walk away, don't run. Dogs like to chase moving things.

If you really feel you are in danger because of this dog, call out loudly for help. If the dog tries to bite you, keep calling out. If you have something small enough, throw it so the dog could be distracted into chasing it. Then you can get away into a store or other safe place. Remember what the dog looks like in case the police need to know. They should know about a stray dog who may be capable of hurting people.

IF YOU SPILL SOMETHING, tell Mom or Dad you're sorry and you want to help clean it up. If your parents aren't home, get paper towels or a big towel from the bathroom or kitchen.

Press a dry towel into the wet part to sop up the spill. Pick up the wet towels and put them in the sink. Then get a clean towel. Wet it with cool water and rub it on the area. Don't use soap or any other cleaner in the house. Sometimes soap or other things you use to clean a stain can make it worse. Cool water is the best cleaner.

Tell your parents what happened as soon as one of them gets home. Tell them what you did to help.

IF SOMEONE STOPS YOU AND DEMANDS YOU GIVE HIM MONEY, stay calm. Give him the money. It's not worth getting hurt even if it makes you feel very angry. If the person threatens to hurt you, give him what he wants and let him go his own way. Muggers are usually in a big hurry. Try to remember what the mugger looked like, and as soon as you can, tell a policeman and your parents about what happened.

There are some good rules to follow so you are safer on the streets.

1. Stay in a group of kids when you're outside. Muggers sometimes look for people who are walking alone.

2. If you are walking alone, keep your head up and your eyes open. Try to watch what's going on around you more than usual. Walk a little faster than you usually do. And walk on busy, well-lit streets whenever you can. Dark, lonely streets make it easier for muggers to surprise people.

3. Cross the street if you have a bad feeling about a person coming near you.

4. If you think you are in danger, duck into a store or the post office or someplace where there will be people. If the person follows you, tell someone or start yelling. Muggers do not want to be noticed.

5. If you're going to school or playing outside, don't wear jewelry or your best clothes. If you need to carry money, carry some in the bottom of each sock and a smaller amount in your pocket. That way, you can give the mugger the smaller amount and tell him that's all you have so he'll go away.

Some people who ask you for money are beggars, not muggers. A beggar does not threaten you when he asks for money. Sometimes a beggar may tell you the money is for a good cause, such as saving baby seals or helping hungry people. No matter how kind this person seems or how good his reasons sound, do not stop. Do not give him any money. Try not to even look the beggar in the eye. Just walk away quickly.

Always tell Mom and Dad what happened so they can tell the police and help you in other ways. Always remember that it's much more important to be safe than to hang onto your money or belongings.

IF A STRANGER OFFERS YOU CANDY, A RIDE, OR A TOY, don't say anything. Just get away from the person as quickly as you can. Sometimes a stranger will ask you to help look for a lost puppy or kitten to try to trick you. No matter how nice the person sounds or what he or she says to you that sounds like fun or something good, just get away. If he says that one of your parents or your brother got hurt and he is going to take you to them, get away. Even if he asks you for some kind of help, get away.

Remember, it's always good to stay with a group of kids when you're outside, at the movies or at a park. It's not a good idea to go to a public bathroom alone. Ask a friend to go with you and both of you keep your eyes open. If you feel that someone is following you, don't stop to make sure. Go where there are other people as fast as you can. Go into a store or office and ask for help. Try to find out ahead of time where the safe places are in the neighborhood. If there is no one around, yell for help. It may scare the person away.

Always tell your parents if a stranger tried to talk to you. Try to remember what the person looked like and where you were at the time. Talk with Mom and Dad about what you should do if a stranger comes near you again.

IF SOMEONE OFFERS YOU DRUGS, ALCOHOL, OR CIGARETTES, calmly say no. Sometimes it's hard to say no. You may like this person or want to do what other kids are doing. Think about what kind of person would want you to do something that could hurt you. People can get seriously sick or die from these things. And a real friend would never want to do that to you.

You never have to explain why you don't want drugs. When you say no without explaining, you let the person know you are not interested at all. He or she will probably leave you alone.

If someone keeps bothering you, tell your parents or a grown-up you know who will help you. When you tell, you are taking an important step toward becoming an adult. You are learning the difference between being a tattletale or crybaby and telling to help somebody.

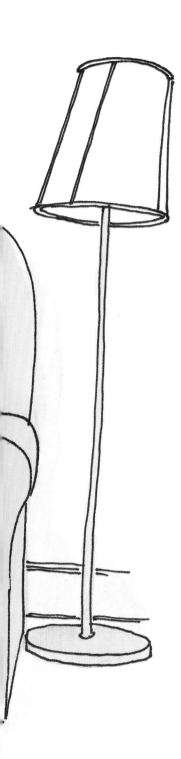

IF SOMEONE TOUCHES YOU IN ANY WAY THAT MAKES YOU FEEL UNCOMFORTABLE, there is more than one thing you can do. First, you can tell the person who touched you that you don't want to be touched like that, even if it is a person you know and like. Tell the person it makes you feel uncomfortable and you don't like it. It is okay to say this and walk away.

Then, tell your mom or dad. Tell them the person's name. Show Mom or Dad what part of your body the person touched or if he hurt you. It is important to tell, because people who touch others in private ways need help so they don't do it anymore.

Sometimes it is tough for grown-ups to believe someone they like could do a bad thing, but you should still tell them. You could also tell a teacher or some other grown-up you trust. To trust someone means you believe he or she will help you.

A very important thing to know is that it is not your fault. Some children think they've done something bad and that's why this happened to them. This is not true. It is part of growing up to learn when to say, "Don't do that," and to ask for help.

If no one listens, you can call a special free phone number for help. It is 1-800-422-4453. You don't know these people, but they are ordinary people like your neighbors who want to make sure you are safe. They volunteer to do this so bad things don't happen to children.

A bully is a person who acts tough and pushes others around so he or she can feel important. A bully has personal problems and takes it out on you. That's sad. He or she needs help. Sometimes a bully is a kid who's scared or lonely or abused.

IF SOMEONE BULLIES YOU, speak calmly to him. Bullies want you to get nervous and upset. If you're calm, you may get a bully to listen to you. He might just be trying to get your attention. Tell him you want to be kind and that you want other people to be kind to you, too.

You may want to hit him back or say something. That never helps though. A bully may feel strong by seeing you squirm. He may get a thrill from it and you may only be making him feel bigger when you do these things.

If the bully won't leave you alone or threatens to hurt you, tell your parents, your teachers or the principal. Let them know you need their help. You may not be able to protect yourself from a bully and his gang if they are dangerous. Don't worry about feeling like a baby. You have a right to be safe.

Normal people try to stay away from troublemakers because they don't like to fight. Talk to adults about how to handle the problem of bullies.

IF YOU GET SEPARATED FROM MOM, DAD, OR THE GROWN-UP TAKING CARE OF YOU, keep your eyes open and stay calm. Think about where you are and what would be the best thing to do.

Most times it's better to stay put. Don't wander off looking for your parents. If you stay in the place you last saw them, they'll probably come back to that spot looking for you.

If you're in a store or shopping mall, go to a person at a cash register and ask for help. Sometimes a policeman or guard in a uniform may be around to help you. It's normal to be afraid when you're lost.

Talk to Mom and Dad ahead of time about what to do if you ever get lost. You can set up a plan for what to do. Having a plan can help you think clearly, be safer, and get back together faster.

IF YOU ARE HOME ALONE AND SOMEONE COMES TO THE DOOR, don't open it, even if the person looks official like a policeman or mailman. If you can, look out the window or through the peephole to see who it is. Never let a stranger know you're home alone. If you have to say something, say your dad is busy right now. But the best think to do is not to say anything and keep the door locked. Most of the time, the stranger will go away.

If the stranger doesn't go away, call Mom or Dad or a neighbor you trust. Someone may be able to come right over and see that the stranger goes away. If no one you call is in, call the police. Have the number by the phone at all times. Tell them about the stranger and make sure you give your address so they can find you.

IF YOU'RE HOME ALONE AND SOMEONE YOU DON'T KNOW VERY WELL CALLS FOR MOM OR DAD, don't tell them they're not home. Say they can't come to the phone right now.

Then ask the caller for his name and phone number. Write the information down and tell the caller Mom or Dad will call back.

IF YOU REALLY WANT SOMETHING AND DON'T GET IT, you will probably be very disappointed. Being disappointed is a very tough thing, especially if you've prayed, promised to be good, or wished very hard.

Disappointment is part of everyone's life. Nobody gets everything they want, and things happen all the time that can result in some kind of difficulty, like an accident or a terrible storm that destroys a forest. It's a big disappointment when things don't go well or the way you expected them to go. Maybe you didn't get the birthday present you were hoping for or you didn't get to go to a ball game because you got the flu.

Remember this: If you can't control or change a situation, sometimes you just have to accept the disappointment. You can change how you think about it, and you probably can take some action to help in some way afterward. Try to turn disappointment into something good. It may be possible if you use your head. For example, if your family vacation had to be canceled, maybe you can arrange to visit a relative or friends during that time. If you've been disappointed with a lower grade than you thought you'd get, it couldn't hurt to discuss it with your teacher. Find out if you can do an extra credit project or get some tutoring.

Because no one can avoid disappointment, learn to make the best of all the curve balls life throws at all of us. Sometimes the only thing you can do is let the situation go and move on to another activity or event.

IF A CLASSMATE WANTS YOU TO CHEAT ON A TEST, cover your paper and say no. Cheating is wrong. The thing about cheating is that, if you help someone with an answer, you are a cheater, too. It doesn't matter whether you gave the answer or asked for it. A person who asks you for answers or asks you to help him see your test paper is not a friend. A real friend would be honest and would want you to be honest.

You could get in trouble at school, too. If you give a friend an answer, you may be helping him or her get a good score on a test, but your friend is learning the bad habit of counting on someone else to bail him out of a tough spot.

Think about what kind of adult a person who cheats may become. Maybe he or she will be dishonest in other ways.

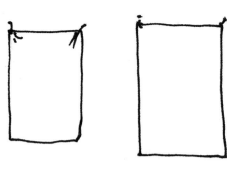

IF YOU NEED HELP WITH YOUR SCHOOLWORK, it's okay to ask for help. You may feel embarrassed and shy about telling your parents or teacher you're having trouble. The work can be very hard for you, but that does not mean you are stupid. You may just need to slow down and concentrate. To concentrate means to think about the work and not think about anything else at that time. It's hard to concentrate if there is a lot going on around you or if your mind is on something else, like a new puppy or band practice.

Sometimes you may feel the teacher is going too fast. And a teacher who *wants* to teach you many things can get annoyed when a student doesn't pay attention. Teachers aren't perfect and students aren't perfect either. After class, you can go to the teacher and say politely, "I know you have a tough job and it's not easy to explain things, but I'd like to hear it one more time."

If you still don't understand, you can say, "Sometimes I'm so confused that I don't know what questions to ask." You should let your teacher know you are trying your best. Perhaps you and your teacher can have a talk and solve the problem. Remember that teachers are supposed to help you learn; it's their job. Most of them decided to be teachers because they want to help you.

One of the best ways to get help is to ask a friend or an older brother or sister to explain what you don't understand.

You should also find out if you're having trouble in school because you can't see or hear well. You may need to have your eyes or ears checked. Sometimes kids have a hard time with schoolwork because of a simple problem that can be solved. Go to the school nurse and find out if your eyes and ears can be checked there. Don't feel embarrassed. Lots of kids need glasses or a tiny hearing aid.

Remember, each person has different talents and gifts. Focus on your special abilities every way you can, and don't worry that you can't be good at everything.

IF YOU LOSE A GAME OR FAIL A TEST, you may feel you're not as good as a person who won or did well. You may feel so upset that you want to cry. That's a normal feeling. Nobody likes to do poorly. Plenty of famous people failed at things, but that didn't stop them from trying again and again. All the big baseball stars have struck out. Everyone can make mistakes. The trick is to learn from your mistakes and get yourself back into gear as soon as you can.

It could be that you didn't do all you could have done to make sure you were ready for a test. Or you really didn't play your best game. Next time you might put more effort into getting ready. Then you can feel good that you've put out your best effort.

Take all that energy you're spending feeling sorry for yourself and turn it into energy for practicing or studying more. Think about what you want to be good at and picture yourself doing it. It's important to be positive and to keep trying.

HOME 2

VISITOR 6

IF YOU ARE SO AFRAID OF BUGS, HIGH PLACES, OR SOME OTHER THING THAT IT MAKES YOUR HEART POUND HARD OR MAKES YOU ILL, the best thing to do is start talking about it with your parents, your teacher, or a friend. Telling someone can be a big relief and lets you know you are not the only one with this kind of problem.

People can feel afraid of many things that can hurt them, like a speeding car or bees flying nearby. Being afraid is healthy when it helps you think of ways to protect yourself.

But sometimes people learn to be afraid of things that really can't hurt them. They become afraid of getting into an elevator, of high places, or even of a neighbor's cat. Sometimes you can teach yourself to get over being afraid of something little by little.

If you fear cats, try looking at cat pictures in a book for just a minute. The next day, look at them for two minutes. Keep going until you can look at them for quite a while without feeling upset. Then try looking at a real cat or going into the same room with one for a short period. Maybe Mom or Dad will go with you so you're not so scared. Eventually, try petting the cat's head for a second. You may find you're not afraid anymore, and the cat is nice and gentle.

Sometimes you can remember something that has happened that made you afraid. Try to figure out what scares you about a thing. It won't make sense to try to pet a bug or snake, but reading interesting things about such creatures may teach you many of them are harmless. Step-by-step, you can learn not to be *that* scared.

If you are afraid to leave your house, go to school, or do things kids normally do, your mom and dad may want you to talk things over with a psychologist or other special counselor. A psychologist is a special doctor who helps you get over your unhealthy fears.

Many times you can help yourself. But when you try to solve a problem yourself and still can't do it, you shouldn't be afraid to ask for help from others who care about you. If you think other people will laugh or think you're weak or silly, that's not true. Everyone is afraid of something. It is very grown-up to admit to being afraid of something instead of hiding it.

IF YOU ARE BLAMED FOR SOMETHING YOU DIDN'T DO, speak up. Tell the adults or others involved that you are an honest person and that, even though it may look like you did something bad, you did not. Tell them they've made a mistake. It's normal to feel very angry. You may not even know who is really to blame for doing the bad thing. You may wonder how anyone could believe a bad thing about you, too. You may even feel it is difficult to make the others believe what you're telling them.

That's why it is very important to try to stay clear of trouble. If you play with kids who get into mischief, you're bound to do something mischievous sooner or later. It may even seem okay because your friends are doing it, too, but if you go along with them, you are using bad judgment.

IF YOU ARE PUNISHED FOR DOING SOMETHING WRONG, you may feel very angry and upset. That's normal. Think about why you were punished. What should you have done instead? Adults who care about you want to teach you what they think is right. If you learn these lessons, you will gain their trust and be able to do many things on your own. They have to know how you will act when you are alone. When you choose to do the wrong thing, you are letting them know you are still too immature to be trusted. Doing the right thing is always your choice. When you decide to stick with the right action, you are growing up.

Sometimes adults may feel you don't listen. So sending you to your room or saying you can't watch TV for a week is the only way to get your attention. If you think you should not have been punished, talk to your parents. Tell them what you think would have been fair and try to solve the problem together. Make sure you listen to what your parents and teachers tell you. They want you to grow up to be happy and to get along with many kinds of people.

IF YOU WANT TO CHANGE BAD BEHAVIOR AND NEED HELP WITH SELF-CONTROL, first identify the behavior and how you want to be different. Talk honestly with your teacher and your parents about the problem, whether it's fighting in school, forgetting your homework, or anything you feel is out of control. They may recommend a good counselor who could help you.

Practice self-control. For example, blow bubbles and calmly watch them drift away. Learn not to give in to being destructive or negative. Replace bad behavior with good behavior. Instead of punching a wall when you're angry, punch your pillow. Then talk to an adult about what made you so angry. Instead of being late for school every day, set your alarm for an earlier wake-up time. Remember, you can change bad behavior if you own up to it and want to fix it.

Self-control is a very important skill in life. The best athletes, performers, and successful people practice excellent self-control. You always need to control yourself in some way or other. Self-control helps you think clearly, make good decisions, and act right.

WHEN YOU SAY YOU'RE BORED, you are insulting your own imagination. You could probably think of a hundred things to do even if you were alone in an empty room. But if you just wait for something fun to drop in your lap, it probably won't happen.

If you're bored, one of the best things to do is read. Find an interesting book in the library or at home. If it's a storybook, try reading it aloud in a dramatic voice, and imagine you are on stage telling the story to an audience. A book can take you to foreign lands and introduce you to characters you would never otherwise meet. If it's a book that tells you how to do something like make a cake, ask Mom or Dad if you can try the recipe.

Why not try something called brainstorming? That means you and your friends think of many ideas. Some of them will probably be zany, but some could be fun and safe. Then maybe you could do one of the things you've thought of yourselves.

Here's one idea. You can make your own picture book with drawings or cutouts from old magazines. Try doing an "All About Me" book. Write about the things you do, what you look like, and what you think you'll be like when you're grown up. Paste or draw pictures on the pages, too. Then you can make a book cover with two pieces of cardboard that you've decorated. Make some holes down the side of the cardboard covers and all the pages and put string through them.

If you do this project with a friend, you can read each other's book and learn a lot about each other.

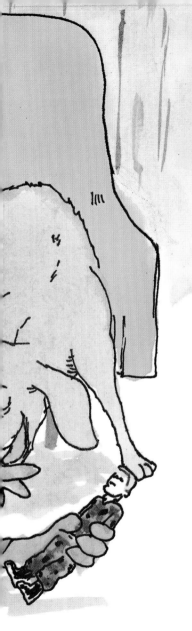

IF YOU HAVE A FIGHT WITH YOUR BROTHER OR SISTER, you probably feel very mad. You may even feel like shouting or hitting that person. It's normal to have these feelings at times, but shouting and hitting are NOT the best things to do when you're angry. Instead, when you get mad at someone, count to 10. That will give you time to think.

Words can hurt as badly as being hit. But hurting someone because he's hurt you only makes things worse. Maybe your brother or sister had a tough day or wants to make himself or herself feel strong by attacking you. You can show you are very grown-up by ignoring some nasty comment.

If you are older than your brother or sister, you can be the one who stops the fight. Then you can be proud of yourself for being strong and kind.

IF YOUR PARENTS ARE HAVING AN ARGUMENT, remember that everybody gets angry sometimes. No one likes loud talking and being angry. But grown-ups do argue once in a while, and it's not your fault.

Stay clear of the argument. Let Mom and Dad be alone so they can settle the problem. Even though arguing makes everyone feel uncomfortable, it means two people are still talking to each other and trying to work out their problems. It is not good when people stop talking to each other and just stay mad. Even people who love each other very much argue. That's because no two people are exactly the same. They have to work to make sure they don't bottle up their feelings. It is never good to hold onto anger.

After a while, you can tell Mom and Dad that when they argue, you feel upset. Most of the time, they will tell you not to worry. Grown-ups have ways of solving their problems.

IF YOU DON'T LIKE BEING THE YOUNGER BROTHER OR SISTER, you're like a lot of other kids. It can be hard to be the youngest, especially when your big brother or sister gets to do something you're not allowed to do yet.

But think of some of the special attention you get just because you're the youngest one. You are lucky to be the youngest because you have a brother or sister you can play with and really share your feelings with. It wasn't so long ago that they were little, too.

It may seem like a long time, but you're only little for a few years. Make a list of all your favorite things. Then make another list of all the things you want to have and do when you're older.

If you think people don't listen to you because you are young, it may be true. There are lots of ways to let someone know what you feel is important. You can tell Mom or Dad that even though you are young, you have ideas. You can add something to their talks at dinner or tell them your opinions, too. An opinion is the way you think about something.

If you feel upset—and sometimes that's natural—talk to Mom or Dad about it. They may understand and help you and your older brother or sister get along better.

It may help you to know that many kids don't like being the *older* brother or sister, or the *middle* brother or sister. Every age group has its own problems, so try to understand that you're not the only one. Instead of focusing on difficulties with each other, focus on how lucky you are to have each other. Brothers and sisters are people you will know and love throughout your entire life, and that's a blessing.

IF YOUR PARENTS ARE GETTING A DIVORCE, you may feel very sad, angry, upset, and disappointed. Everything that you know will be changing and it doesn't seem fair. It's a hard time for the whole family. When a mom and dad just can't get along with each other, a divorce may help them feel happier. They don't want to feel angry or hurt all the time. Sometimes they have problems that won't go away no matter how hard they try to solve them. Remember that your parents' problem is not your fault. Some kids think they did something to cause the divorce. Or they feel that their parents are angry with them. But most of the time, parents will tell you they love you and will take care of you even if they don't live together. Your mom will still be your mom and your dad will still be your dad.

Some kids may think that their parents have messed up their lives. It may help to know that your mom or dad probably hurt very badly inside. Most grown-ups work very hard to keep their families together, but a split sometimes happens. Also, your parents thought long and hard before making this decision. They may feel it is best even though it hurts.

Talking about your feelings can be a big help. Sharing how you feel with a friend or grown-up you trust may help you get over thinking about the divorce all the time. No matter how bad you feel at first, you will feel better after a while. It may take time.

You may want to visit a library for books that explain more about divorce. The librarian can show you where to find them.

IF A FRIEND DOESN'T WANT TO BE YOUR FRIEND ANYMORE, it can make you feel very sad and alone. This happens to many kids. There are a lot of reasons. This happens to many kids. There are a lot of reasons. Maybe your friend has found another person to have fun with. Maybe the things you used to do together are not what your friend wants to do now. Or maybe it's just tough to see each other because of homework or new activities like volleyball practice.

This friend may not want to be mean to you, but you may feel hurt anyway. Talk with someone you trust about your feelings. You may want to say bad things about your friend, but that never helps and can make you feel worse. Instead, ask someone if he or she ever lost a friend and what you can do about it.

You can also ask someone you haven't been friends with to play with you. That person may turn out to be a lot of fun. Then you'll have a new friend, too.

It's always hard when you like someone more than he or she likes you. Especially when you have been good friends. Just remember that you are special in your own unique way.

It's normal for friendships to change as people grow up. Try to understand that all people change, and we don't always know why. Recognize that you can't control how another person feels. It's best to let go when a person needs to move on. You may be the one who needs to move on someday, and you may be the one who has to tell someone you can't continue the friendship. Think of how you outgrew the clothes you wore two years ago. People can outgrow one another, which is not necessarily a bad thing. It happens throughout our lives and may actually help us become better individuals.

Having your own house key is a very grown-up responsibility. IF YOU CARRY YOUR HOUSE KEY, wear it around your neck on a chain or keep it someplace where you'll always have it handy. Make sure you can tuck the key out of sight. That way no one can see it and think you'll be home alone.

Make sure your name and address are not on the key. If you lose it, whoever finds it won't know where you live or be able to get into your house. Always check to make sure you have your key before you leave the house. When you get home, lock the door and put the key in the same place every time so you'll know exactly where to find it the next day.

If you lose your key and can't get into the house, go to the house of an adult you trust. You can call your parents from there and wait until someone gets home to open the door.

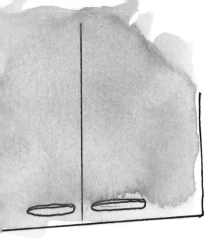

IF YOU BREAK SOMETHING, put on an old pair of gloves. Then carefully put the pieces in a paper bag. Someone may be able to put the pieces back together.

If you break a glass or dish, there may be tiny pieces on the floor. Make sure you have your shoes on. Don't try to pick up tiny pieces with your fingers. Get a dishcloth and gently push the pieces into a bag. If pieces are on the floor, brush them into a bag or dustpan with a broom or handle brush.

If you are afraid you might get cut, leave the broken glass, close the door behind you, and let Mom or Dad know what happened. Ask what else you can do to help.

IF SOMEONE YOU LOVE DIED, it is normal to be sad and cry. It probably will help to talk about your feelings or about the person who died.

Sometimes you may feel that it is your fault the person died. Maybe you think if you had behaved better or listened more, the person wouldn't have died.

This is not true!

It is not your fault.

No one likes to think about sickness, accidents, or bad things that can happen to people. Even grown-ups get very upset when someone dies. Death is the saddest thing in the whole world. Understanding why someone died is difficult. When people die, their family and friends may also feel angry. They feel angry because a person they loved cannot come back—no matter what. It doesn't seem fair. Sometimes they feel afraid that they might die, too.

If you have lost someone who was very special, you should know that other people are there to help you. Talking to your priest, minister, or rabbi may help you. Write down some of your memories of the person who died, or gather photographs that show happy times with that person. You could share these with your family.

Remember that life is a special gift.

The person who died would want you to be happy.

IF A FRIEND TELLS YOU A SECRET, try to keep it a secret. He or she is trusting you to keep important feelings or events private. It is a very special bond to know a secret and keep it. You may hurt a friend if you tell something personal to others. Think about how bad you'd feel if someone told your secret all over town.

Sometimes someone will tell you a "secret" when she is really afraid to come right out and ask for help. A friend may tell you something troublesome and ask you not to tell anybody. If you feel deep down that keeping this kind of secret could hurt, tell it to a grown-up you trust. That means someone who will understand and really try to help.

Explain to your friend that you care about her. She should know that you will be her friend no matter what, and you're going to help with her problem as best you can.

IF YOUR FRIENDS ARE DOING SOMETHING YOU THINK IS WRONG, tell them to stop or get away from them. There are times when a game can get out of hand or when your friends go wild. If they're in your house and your parents aren't home, things may get broken and someone may get hurt. Tell everyone to leave.

If they won't listen to you, call an adult you trust right away and ask for help. If no one is home, go to a neighbor's house and ask an adult to help you handle the problem.

Settle ahead of time with your parents the question of who may play at your house. They'll tell you whether or not they want you to have company when they're not home. It's easier to stay out of trouble in the first place than it is to stop trouble that's already started.

When your friends behave badly, they are showing they don't have respect for your feelings or things. They could get you into serious trouble, too. Keep in mind how terrible you'd feel if someone ripped your sofa or knocked over your TV set or got mud all over the place. Kids who do disrespectful things need help. They have to learn to control themselves.

One of the most dangerous things kids can do is to play with guns. Some parents have guns in the house, but they are not toys and not to be handled by children. Many tragic accidents have happened because children played with a gun or took a gun to school. NO GUN SHOULD EVER BE BROUGHT TO SCHOOL. If you know any child who has a gun, report it immediately to the teacher and principal. If you know any child who says he wants to shoot people, tell your teacher or principal. This child may need help very badly, and others have the right to be protected from harm.

Make the right choice: NEVER PLAY WITH A GUN OR STAY IN THE COMPANY OF A CLASSMATE OR FRIEND WHO HAS A GUN. Get away as soon and as fast as you can.

IF YOU WANT TO GIVE SOMEONE A PRESENT BUT DON'T HAVE ANY MONEY, think about what a gift really is. A gift tells someone you like him and that he is special. When you give a person a present, it should come from your heart. Some presents don't cost any money at all.

You can write Dad a long letter and include your own drawings. You could surprise him by polishing his shoes all shiny. That's one way to say you care enough to give a little bit of yourself.

Sometimes the best gifts are unexpected. You could give someone something of yours even if it isn't new. If you think it is special, there's a good chance the other person will know how much this means to you. Make sure you really want the other person to have it and that he or she would really like it.

Think about writing a poem or giving Mom or Dad 5 tickets for household chores you'll do to help out even more than usual. You'll figure out lots of good things to do.

If you feel embarrassed that a present that doesn't come from a store isn't good enough, think again. People appreciate the thoughtful things you do much more than store-bought presents.

It's not very nice when one of your playmates says something mean to you. Your feelings may get hurt. You may even want to say something mean back. But the grown-up thing to do is much better than that. IF SOMEONE SAYS SOMETHING THAT HURTS YOUR FEELINGS, such as "What an ugly dress," you could say, "Too bad you think so," or "Think whatever you want." Being honest lets the other person know she's being rude.

Another way to deal with someone who says something mean to you is to laugh and pretend you agree. That way the person wouldn't get the thrill she was looking for. Chances are people who insult others enjoy making them upset and angry. If you don't act upset or angry, she'll probably leave you alone. If you act strong, she may gain new respect for you.

Sometimes people say mean things to make themselves feel big or more important. That's sad, because that usually means a person has a low opinion of himself. Saying something mean to another is childish and doesn't help. A very wise person once said no one can really insult you unless you *allow* the insult to affect you in a bad way. When you think about it, it's true. If you decide you won't let someone's mean words do you harm, they won't. Sometimes it's best to ignore a mean remark.

Also, there may be a time when someone insults you but he or she is really a good friend and may not have meant to hurt your feelings. You can say, "What you said isn't very kind. It hurt my feelings." You may want to ask why he or she hurt your feelings. Everyone says something nasty to another person every once in a while, and that's normal. Just remember to patch things up, say you're sorry, and think twice before you say something you shouldn't.

Have you ever known a person who had more toys than you or had something you wish you had? Or was smarter? Or played basketball better than you? If you ever felt bad that you didn't have something that someone else had, you are like many people. Everyone feels jealous sometimes.

IF YOU FEEL JEALOUS, make a list of all the great things you have had. Maybe you have a soft pillow that's just right. Maybe you have a grandparent who tells you the best stories ever. Or maybe you got to ride a horse or swim at the beach this summer.

Here's something you can do with a friend. Make a list of things you want to have and do when you grow up. Have lots of fun. See how different the lists you come up with are and draw pictures to go with them.

It's nice to have a lot of things, but remember that good things are not always from the store.

If you have the feeling that you never get anything you really need, you may have a serious situation. You should talk to your parents or another trusted adult about this before you become depressed or terribly angry. Situations can always change when people know how you feel.

IF YOU WOULD RATHER NOT DO CHORES IN THE HOUSE, put on the radio or stereo and just get busy cleaning up. Everyone in your house who's old enough should help Mom and Dad clean up. Mom and Dad need your help with housework because they have a great deal of work to do. Think of everything they do: work at their jobs, go to the supermarket, cook, do laundry, take care of you, and a lot more.

Most people would rather be doing something other than cleaning up. It takes time away from other fun things we would rather be doing. But cleaning up is everyone's responsibility. You live in the house, so it is only fair to help out. How about making up a game like, "Your favorite sports star will be here in an hour." It can help the job go much faster.

You should know that dirt, dust, and clutter can breed germs and bugs. It's a good idea to learn about germs and how you can avoid them. Ask your parents or teacher to explain what germs are. One thing you'll find out is that good old soap and water can keep germs from growing.

It's a good feeling to have everything clean and in good order.

IF SOMEONE WANTS YOU TO TELL A LIE, tell that person you don't lie about things. Lying is like cheating. It can cause you a lot of problems.

Usually a person who lies is trying to get out of a tough situation. It is a bad habit. It might get you out of trouble that one time, but it is a weak thing to do. You may be surprised that your Mom and Dad are proud of you when you tell the truth. They know they can rely on what you tell them. This is the way they grow to trust you and let you do more things on your own.

It's much easier to tell the truth. And you'll feel good about yourself, too. You'd want others to be honest with you, too. Think how terrible you'd feel if a friend told you a lie and you found out.

If you've done something you shouldn't, admit you were wrong even if you know you'll be punished. You get hurt the most by lying. Lying is taking the easy way out. It can make you feel guilty inside and hurt other people.

IF YOUR BABY-SITTER DOES SOMETHING YOU THINK IS WRONG, it's important to tell Mom and Dad. Don't think you're being a tattletale.

A baby-sitter is someone who's supposed to be responsible for you when your parents are out. The baby-sitter has an important job to do. If he or she invites a friend to your house, drinks alcohol, uses drugs, or tells you to do weird things, then that baby-sitter is not doing his or her job. You could get hurt if your baby-sitter can't protect you as he or she is supposed to do. You should tell your parents if the baby-sitter is using something in the house you think he or she shouldn't use or if you have a problem with the baby-sitter.

Your parents will only know what is going on if you tell them. They hire a baby-sitter because they want to know you are safe and being taken care of. Both you and your parents will feel better if you are being cared for by someone you trust.

IF YOU SOMETIMES WISH BAD THINGS WOULD HAPPEN TO SOMEONE ELSE, your imagination is at work. Imagining means thinking about things that are not always real. Usually, imagining things is healthy and normal.

Sometimes it can get out of hand. Think about why you want something bad to happen. Has someone hurt your feelings? Or not let you go somewhere you wanted? It may help to think about why the person did what he or she did.

It's hard to look at the other side of things when you're upset. It seems unfair. But you'll be smarter if you try to understand.

Then think about something good and get busy doing something that is fun. If you still feel bothered, tell Mom, Dad, or your teacher what's on your mind. He or she may be able to answer your questions and help you not to worry. If you keep it to yourself, you may get more upset. Remember, bad things don't happen just because you imagine them.

If you think about bad things happening to others all the time or if you do things to make bad things happen, talk to someone who cares about you. You may be very angry or tense deep down and need help to sort out those feelings.

IF YOU ARE SICK AND HAVE TO STAY AT HOME, settle in until you feel better. Getting sick is no fun. Most people hate to stay in bed, take medicine, and do what the doctor says. You may have to miss a party or something you wanted to do. Most of the time you only have to stay in bed for a couple of days. You can watch your favorite TV shows, have some special things to eat, and read an exciting book.

You can also think about getting well. Make a list of things you want to do when you're okay again. That can help your body to feel better.

IF YOU HAVE TO GO TO THE HOSPITAL, ask Mom or Dad to take you there before you have to stay overnight. Then you can see the nurses and see what your room will be like. It won't seem so scary if you ask questions and talk about what will happen when you get to the hospital. Tell Mom and Dad you'd like to know ahead of time.

Sometimes, someone gets hurt or sick and has to be taken to the hospital right away. If this happens to you, try to stay calm. Remember that doctors and nurses at the hospital know what to do to help you and they care about making you better. The hospital is a place where you can get more help than any place else.

It's normal to feel afraid of shots or taking medicine. It may be the first time you've slept away from home or had people examine you.

The important thing to know is that you want to get better, and that may mean being uncomfortable for a while. Find out when your parents can visit you. Talk to a grown-up you trust about your feelings. Sharing your problems can make them seem a little smaller.

IF YOU HAVE TO WEAR BRACES ON YOUR TEETH OR GET GLASSES, you may feel funny about how you look at first. You may think you look silly or ugly, but most of the time that's not true. Many children have to wear braces so their teeth will be straight when they are older. You don't have to wear braces forever. The time you do wear them may seem long, but it will be over soon.

And count all the people who wear glasses! Ask Mom or Dad to help you pick out glasses that look good on your face and will be fun to wear. Remember how important it is to see clearly. Glasses help you do just that. After a while, you'll get used to them, and so will your friends. When you're old enough, you may be able to wear contact lenses.

It's not easy getting used to a different face in the mirror. Braces and glasses are two examples of things that can change the way you look at yourself. Many times the change is for a short time. If the change is permanent, you'll probably feel better for it in the long run. There might even be a time when you think you look funny *without* glasses. You will get used to your new look after a while.

IF THUNDER AND LIGHTNING SCARE YOU, get busy reading, drawing, or doing something you like to do. Pet your dog or cat. Help Mom make cookies. Play a game with your family. If you're home alone, you might even want to just listen to the storm. The sounds don't have to be frightening. They can also be fascinating.

To keep safe during a very bad storm, stay indoors and don't use anything electrical or play in water. The electricity in lightning is attracted to water and electrical appliances. Keep windows and doors closed. The telephone runs on electricity, too, so it is a good idea not to use it when there is lightning. If there isn't any lightning, calling a friend may help you feel calmer, or you can watch TV or listen to music.

If you do get caught outside in a thunderstorm, try to find shelter. If there are no buildings around, find a low place and stay there. Don't stay under a tree, because high and tall things attract lightning.

A storm is usually just a lot of rain and loud noise. Most thunder and lightning can't hurt you, but electricity is dangerous and you should be careful during an electrical storm.

IF YOU WORRY ABOUT GETTING A DISEASE OR SOMEONE YOU LOVE GETTING SICK, you might feel better if you knew more about the disease or what could happen. Many times it is a germ that causes a disease. Germs can cause serious illnesses like cancer and AIDS, but they can cause minor sicknesses like colds, too.

Ask your school nurse or teacher to explain about germs. She may tell you it's not a good idea to be close to someone with a cold, share your drinking glass or straw, or touch someone else's skin when it's bleeding. Germs can spread when you share a piece of food, like an ice-cream cone or apple, especially if your mouth touches the food. Germs live everywhere, but you can make it less comfortable for them by keeping yourself and your home clean. Washing your hands a lot is a good idea, too.

If you worry about getting sick, you may want to go to the library. You will be able to find out how people get diseases and what you do to make sure your body is as healthy and strong as it can be.

Talking to a nurse, your family doctor, or a grown-up you trust about how you feel may help you worry less about getting sick.

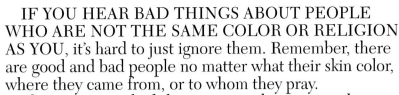

IF YOU HEAR BAD THINGS ABOUT PEOPLE WHO ARE NOT THE SAME COLOR OR RELIGION AS YOU, it's hard to just ignore them. Remember, there are good and bad people no matter what their skin color, where they came from, or to whom they pray.

If a person says bad things to you about your color or religion, the best thing to do is walk away. It's sad when other people try to hurt your feelings because of these things. They haven't taken the time to find out what you are like before they make up their minds. They think they know all about people like you and don't bother to find out for themselves.

You should feel sorry for people with such small minds. Think about some of the things they'll never know. Maybe your mom makes a cake that only comes from your parents' country or you can speak two languages instead of one. You have something no one else has. No matter what any bully says, he can't take these things from you.

People say mean things for many reasons. Some want to make you feel low because you are not the same as they are or they're afraid of different people. Your ways or looks, even your food, may seem strange to them. These people feel threatened by people and things that are different from them. You are lucky because you know about two cultures, not just one. (Culture is the way a person lives and what he or she believes.) Everyone can learn from each other and share new thoughts and ways.

It is a bad habit to call people who are different from you bad names. Remember, if everyone were exactly the same, the world would be a pretty boring place. Try to understand why you lash out at a person or a group. Have you heard bad things about these people? Have you picked up an attitude from friends or others that you are better than some groups of people? Prejudice is a type of hatred that hurts two people. Mostly, though, it hurts the person who hates because it closes his mind. That would be a terrible thing to do to yourself.

IF YOU ARE GOING TO MOVE TO A NEW HOUSE OR NEIGHBORHOOD, you may feel happy and sad at the same time. You may feel excited because there will be a new house and neighborhood to get to know. But you may also feel sad because you have to leave your friends.

Change is a part of life. Moving often means saying good-bye to the places and people you know. But it also means you'll be learning all about a new place and people. You can write letters to your best friends about your new school. Maybe you can send pictures or drawings of the new place. They can write to you and tell you what they're doing.

Sometimes moving can be hard, but it is exciting to have new experiences. Learning new things is fun. You may feel shy at first or uncomfortable at being the "new kid." But in a little while, you'll get to know your new teachers and classmates. Soon, you will be very much at home. And there will be another "new kid" for you to get to know.

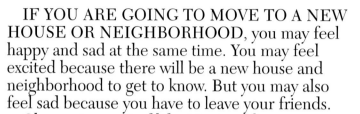

IF YOU HAVE A NIGHTMARE, you wake up scared with your heart pounding. Everyone has nightmares once in a while. A nightmare is like seeing or being in a scary movie while you're asleep. But just remember, it was only a bad dream. It is not real.

Some people believe you can have a nightmare if you eat too late or watch a horror movie or hear something bad on the news. All these things can upset you. Others think nightmares happen when you feel nervous or if something is worrying you. No one knows for sure where nightmares come from, but the best thing you can do is talk about the nightmare with a grown-up you trust. Talking can help you figure out what's bothering you deep down and how to take care of it. A hug from Mom or Dad can make you feel a lot better, too.

IF YOU ANSWER THE TELEPHONE and hear a weird voice or someone saying embarrassing things, don't say anything. Hang up the phone. Tell a grown-up about the call.

Some people have problems they don't know how to solve. They do strange things that even they can't explain sometimes. By not answering them back, you let them know they can't scare or hurt you.

IF YOU ARE USING A COMPUTER AND YOU SEE WEIRD THINGS OR GET MESSAGES FROM STRANGERS ASKING YOU ABOUT YOURSELF, report it immediately to your family. Many people with bad and harmful ideas log on to the Internet and try to find young people who will communicate with them. They may ask extremely personal questions. They may ask about sex or about illegal things. If you give these people information about yourself, your family, or your school, you may be in danger. Even if a person sounds nice, you may be setting yourself up for trouble. Internet messages may lead to meeting a person with bad intentions. Never communicate with strangers on the Internet or let them know who and where you are. Refuse to give out any information about your family or friends. Ask your parents to block Internet sites that are dangerous or upsetting to you. If a friend thinks they're okay or fun, tell him or her that's foolish. There are plenty of other ways to have real fun. Friends should help protect one another.

Online sites that show nasty pictures or that advertise pornography should be off-limits to children. Pornography means writing or pictures that are supposed to cause sexual reactions. It is wrong for children to be exposed to this, and it is worse that you could become a victim of it. Don't be afraid to speak up about Internet pornography. Show your parents what you are seeing on the Internet. Protect yourself and other kids. Bad Internet communications can lead to kidnappings, drugs, even murder. Horrible things really can happen because kids log on to certain web sites. They think it's going to be a thrill, but actually they're making themselves easy targets for criminals.

If you are open and honest with your parents and teachers about what you see on the Internet, you are doing yourself and many others a favor. If you feel confused or disturbed by these things, talk it out with an adult. Your parents and teachers can help keep you safe. Computers are wonderful for doing many different tasks, but use your head when it comes to the bad stuff. Beware of people who abuse computer technology in order to commit crimes.

Everyone feels nervous every once in a while. IF YOU FEEL NERVOUS OR ANXIOUS ABOUT SOMETHING THAT'S HAPPENING OR SOMETHING YOU HAVE TO DO, take a slow, deep breath in through your nose. Then blow the air out of your mouth very slowly, like blowing out birthday candles in slow motion. Do this three or four times. Deep breathing gives you some "time out" and helps you think more clearly.

Talking to a grown-up or a close friend about your feelings can help, too. We all get the jitters over little things, but sometimes you feel almost sick with nervousness, especially in a serious situation. If you have to get up in front of the class to give a report, for example, and your heart is pounding and you feel weak or dizzy or terrified, take your time. Get ready to just talk and be yourself. Be prepared to speak. Rehearsing your speech at home ahead of time can help a lot. Knowing exactly what you are going to do or say is the key to success. Once you begin, you'll be fine. If you trip up on a word or a sentence, don't worry about it. Think about this: Even the best news reporters on TV flub their words now and then. It's no big deal.

If you worry that people will laugh at you, just know in your heart that they'll be just as nervous when it's their turn. Many famous actors talk about "stage fright," which means they get nervous before a performance. Think of the Olympic athletes, who often get very nervous and excited about the competition. When they learn to accept their nervousness, they are able to perform well. You can learn to push past your nervous feelings.

If your nervousness happens too often and too severely—that is, if you can't get going at all because you are paralyzed with fear—ask for help from your parents, your teacher, or another adult. Share your feelings and experience: That really can help you feel a lot better very quickly. Remember, many of your classmates and friends have the same anxiety.

IF YOU FEEL AFRAID OF THE DARK, remember that many other people are afraid, too. Even grown-ups. The dark can't hurt you.

Take some deep breaths and close your eyes. Think how peaceful a dark room is. Maybe you can cuddle your favorite Teddy bear or pat your cat's head.

Maybe you see shapes moving in the dark or imagine creatures under the bed. That is your imagination at work. Maybe the next time a dragon rises up, you could imagine a knight spearing him. You could think about something warm like a bunch of newborn puppies squealing and squirming under your bed.

If you are really scared, you can ask Mom or Dad for a little night light for your room. Think about growing up and not being afraid of the dark anymore. That would be nice.

IF YOU FEEL UPSET BY A MOVIE OR TELEVISION SHOW, talk about your feelings with Mom or Dad or a grown-up you trust. When a movie or TV show is about something gloomy or scary, it's normal to feel gloomy or scared because of it. Shows are supposed to be dramatic. The people who create the shows and the actors playing the parts want everything to seem real and exciting to those who watch.

Remember that even if a show seems real to you it's usually just a story for entertainment. The actors are not really getting hurt or killed. They're pretending. When some shows do make you feel concerned after they're over, it's okay to ask questions.

It's also okay not to watch shows that upset or scare you just because your friends are watching them.

Some shows retell true stories. These may make you feel sad, happy, or even angry. That's all right. Just talk about those feelings and don't keep them bottled up.

IF YOU FEEL LONELY because your friends are busy and can't spend time with you right now, get involved with an activity on your own. You can read a good book, put together a puzzle, or build a model airplane. Sometimes it's wonderful to be by yourself. You can think about things you'd like to do. And sometimes new ideas come to you just because you've had time to be alone and think about things.

Plenty of children like to be alone and that's okay.

But if you feel too lonely too much of the time, talk about it with your parents. They may help you figure out why you're feeling sad or uncomfortable. They may even suggest ways to make you feel less shy or unaccepted by others. Maybe you could join a club at school and make some new friends. If it's all right with Mom and Dad, call one of your favorite relatives and ask what he or she would do. You can ask your teacher, too. Many people feel lonely at times.

If you think you are so shy that you are creating loneliness for yourself all the time, remember that we all have personal power to use. Tell yourself you are a good person and have a lot to offer. Tell yourself it's your choice to make friends, take part in activities, and feel good about yourself. Talk to someone!

IF YOU HATE TO TAKE A BATH OR WASH, too bad for you. You would probably feel embarrassed if someone told you that you smelled. Or worse, if people didn't want to be around you or talk with you because you were unpleasant to be close to.

You have to get washed every day, like it or not. You have to brush your teeth, wash your face and hands and the rest of your body, and wear clean clothes. Think of how terrible we'd all smell and look if we didn't clean ourselves! Even animals groom themselves and their babies.

Humans do it better, because we know dirt can cause germs and sickness. It's okay to get dirty when you're out playing. But a bath can be fun and relaxing. Ask Mom to help you find a nice smelling soap or bubble bath or shampoo that won't sting if it gets in your eyes.

You can look forward to being old enough to take showers by yourself. Showers and baths will soon feel very good to you and you'll want to be clean all the time.

Have you ever lost a toy or something you liked very much? That happens to everyone. You look everywhere, but you just can't find it. What should you do IF YOU CAN'T FIND SOMETHING YOU'VE LOST?

Maybe Mom, Dad, or another person in your house has seen it. Someone may help you look. Or you can make believe you are a detective. A detective is a person who thinks very hard and tries to find answers to things.

Think about everything you did when you last had your favorite thing. Think about where you were in the house with it. Did you take it into the living room? Were you holding it when you were talking on the phone? Could it be under the bed or in a book?

No one likes to lose things, but if you can't find it after a while, it's a good time to think about being more careful. And who knows? That special thing may turn up after a while.

IF YOU DON'T LIKE TO EAT VEGETABLES OR TRY NEW FOODS, you could be missing out on something good. You may be missing the foods that will make you grow, make you stronger, and make your brain work better. The foods you eat combine in your body to make it work right. That's called good *nutrition*.

You need to eat foods from four basic food groups. If you want to help your body fight germs and work well, you need vitamins and minerals. You can get them in vegetables like carrots, potatoes, green beans, and more.

If you want to help your muscles and bones grow strong, you need to eat protein. You can get protein in meat, fish, eggs, and beans.

Dairy products like milk and cheese will work to strengthen your bones and teeth.

You need breads and cereals to help your body clean out your insides, get rid of waste material without any trouble, and to give you energy.

Fruit has the vitamins, minerals, and natural sugar to keep you on the go. The fiber in fruits helps flush out all your body waste.

It's also important to drink plenty of water (about six glasses a day) to keep your body working properly.

If you have a certain food you prefer most of the time, you're like a lot of people. But plenty of people also really like salads, different kinds of seafood, and other healthy things to eat. Eating should be a pleasure, but use your head, too. You need a well-balanced diet. Try tasting different foods. You won't know if you like something until you've tried it. If you taste something you don't like, be polite about it. Nobody likes everything.

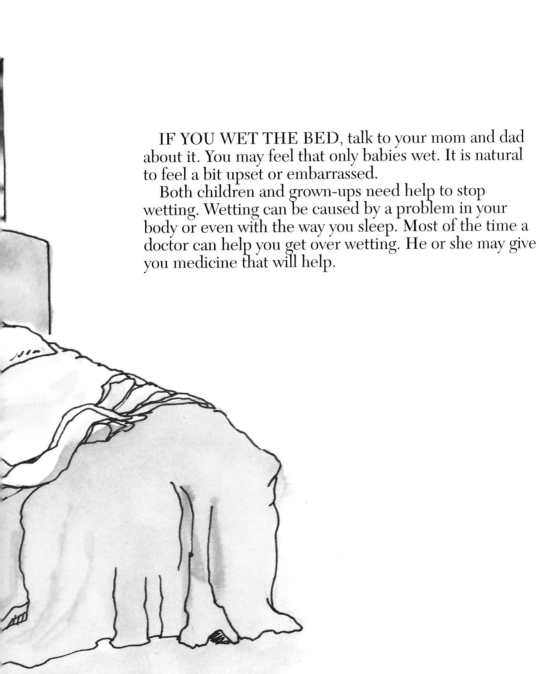

IF YOU WET THE BED, talk to your mom and dad about it. You may feel that only babies wet. It is natural to feel a bit upset or embarrassed.

Both children and grown-ups need help to stop wetting. Wetting can be caused by a problem in your body or even with the way you sleep. Most of the time a doctor can help you get over wetting. He or she may give you medicine that will help.

IF YOU PROMISE TO DO SOMETHING, you are saying you will do it. On your honor. A promise is an important decision, so think carefully before you make one.

People rely on what you promise to do. If you promise to help your sister with homework, she is counting on your being there. What if your best friend promised to meet you after school and then didn't show up? You would be very disappointed.

It's important for people to know they can believe you and can rely on your promise. If you promise to call home when you get somewhere and then don't do it, you could cause a lot of worry. That's not a kind thing to do to your mom and dad.

When you don't do something you've promised, people think they can't trust you. Sometimes it's impossible to keep a promise. If that happens, you could explain to the person what happened. That's not easy either, but at least the person knows you feel bad about it.

TALKING IT OVER:
Things to Talk About with Mom or Dad

Have you and your family ever made plans to give a birthday party or go on a vacation? If so, you probably have an idea of how important it is to get all the details set ahead of time. That way, each of you knows what to do and the plans can go smoothly. Planning makes everything easier.

If you plan ahead, you'll be able to handle a problem or prevent one from happening. Here is a list of things you should talk over with Mom or Dad.

• Ask your parents when you should call them at work, and whom to call in case of an emergency. Make sure you write the numbers down on the last page of this book. Keep this book or a sheet of paper with important phone numbers by the phone.

• Go over how to use the telephone. Mom and Dad can teach you how to call the police, fire department, first-aid squad, emergency services department, or a person they trust to help you when they're not around. Learn how to take and write good messages, too.

• Ask which phone numbers you should learn by heart. In an emergency, you won't have to look them up.

• Find out what your parents expect of you when they're not home. Knowing the house rules ahead of time will help the whole family to cooperate and prevent problems. What are the rules of your house? Can you have friends over when Mom or Dad aren't home? Can you use the oven or other appliances in the kitchen? Make one list for "yes" and one for "no."

• Know your street number, your full name, and the name of your town by heart. Always carry identification with you that tells your name, address, home phone number, and phone numbers for your parents. That way if anything happens to you, someone can let your mom or dad know.

• Ask what you should do if you miss the school bus or arrive too late for an after-school lesson. If you have a plan, chances are you'll be calmer and safer.

Author's Biography—**Tova Navarra**

A magna cum laude graduate of Seton Hall University, registered nurse, and former Copley News Service columnist, Tova Navarra has written more than 20 books, including *The Encyclopedia of Asthma and Respiratory Disorders; Allergies A to Z; The Encyclopedia of Vitamins, Minerals and Supplements; Therapeutic Communication; An Insider's Guide to Home Health Care; Wisdom for Caregivers; Toward Painless Writing: A Guide for Health Professionals; Your Body: Highlights of Human Anatomy; The College History Series: Seton Hall University* and *Monmouth University; Images of America: Levittown, The First Fifty Years; The New Jersey Shore: A Vanishing Splendor,* and others. Formerly the art critic and family writer for the *Asbury Park Press,* Ms. Navarra is currently working on an encyclopedia of alternative medicines and another self-help book for young people. She is profiled in *Who's Who of American Women,* and she lives in Monmouth County, New Jersey.

This book is dedicated to Dr. Phil and Oprah, with love.
Tova

To Mary and Emily, who continue to love me just because I'm me.
Tom

Illustrator's Biography—**Tom Kerr**

Now settled in the Midwest, Tom Kerr has spent his entire career working as an illustrator and graphic designer with a slant on children and learning.

He earned degrees from Williams College and the State College of Victoria (Australia). A self-taught artist, he assembled his portfolio and began his career with freelance and commission assignments while working as a full-time teacher.

Since his return to the United States from Down Under, Mr. Kerr has illustrated more than twenty books, including *Welcome to Dinsmore the World's Greatest Store* and *A Dad's Guide to Babies.* He also illustrates for newspapers and magazines both here and abroad, and is currently drawing McGruff the Crime Dog® for the National Crime Prevention Council in Washington.

He is married, has two cats, and is justifiably proud of his 13-year-old daughter.

INDEX

IMPORTANT PHONE NUMBERS AND INFORMATION
General Emergency: 911*

*In many towns you can call this number for any emergency. You should check to see if your town uses this number.

Emergency Services Department: _____

Police Department: _____

First-Aid Squad: _____

Fire Department: _____

Family Doctor: _____

Poison Control Center: _____

Mom's Office: _____

Dad's Office: _____

Neighbor Who Could Help: _____

Relative: _____

Friend's Mom or Dad Who Could Help:

_____